THE SOURCES OF MY *Essence*

LESTER WITCHER JR.

Copyright © 2023 Lester Witcher Jr.

All rights reserved. No part of this book may be reproduced, stored, or transmitted by any means—whether auditory, graphic, mechanical, or electronic—without written permission of both publisher and author, except in the case of brief excerpts used in critical articles and reviews. Unauthorized reproduction of any part of this work is illegal and is punishable by law.

ISBN: 979-8-88640-974-1 (sc)
ISBN: 979-8-88640-975-8 (hc)
ISBN: 979-8-88640-976-5 (e)

Because of the dynamic nature of the Internet, any web addresses or links contained in this book may have changed since publication and may no longer be valid. The views expressed in this work are solely those of the author and do not necessarily reflect the views of the publisher, and the publisher hereby disclaims any responsibility for them.

One Galleria Blvd., Suite 1900, Metairie, LA 70001
1-888-421-2397

Contents

Chapter 1   Chatter from the Heart.. 1
    Alone 2
    Amazing 3
    As My Heart Cries 6
    Beauty 7
    Creative Souls 8
    Day & Night 10
    Dream Girl 11
    Dreams 12
    First Love (The One That Got Away) 13
    Ghost of Love 14
    Great Picasso 16
    Hands of Time 18
    Heart Erodes 19
    Joy 21
    Mind-Blowing 24
    My Future 25
    My Queen 26
    Pain in My Soul 27
    Part of My Soul 28
    Please God Heal Me 29
    Roots of My Essence 30

Chapter 2   Acknowledgements 33
    Farewell 34
    Grandpa 35
    Sisterly Love 36
    My Brothers 37
    Single Women on Valentine's Day 38

Lovely Feet Valentine's Day 39
Happy Retirement 40
Happy 19th Anniversary 41

Chapter 3   Birthday Celebrations 43
Happy Birthday Shekita 44
Happy Birthday Mom/Grandmom/Great Grandmom 45
Happy Birthday Auntie 2021 46
Happy 50th Birthday Cuz 47
Happy 50th Birthday Dex 48
Happy Birthday Mel 49
Greatness Offering Dreams 50

Chapter 4   Mother's Day 51
Happy Mother's Day to My Daughter 52
Happy Mother's Day Mom 2020 53
Happy Mother's Day Grandmom 2020 54
Happy Mother's Day Auntie 2020 55
Happy Mother's Day Mom 2021 56
Happy Mother's Day Grandmom 2021 57
Happy Mother's Day Auntie 2021 58
Happy Mother's Day Mom 2022 59
Happy Mother's Day Grandmom 2022 60
Happy Mother's Day Auntie 2022 61

Chapter 5   Merry Christmas/Happy New Year 63
Merry Christmas/Happy New Year Mom Lynch 64
Merry Christmas/Happy New Year Kesha 65
Merry Christmas/Happy New Year Tonya 66
Merry Christmas/Happy New Year Mom 67
Merry Christmas/Happy New Year Grandmom 2020 68
Merry Christmas/Happy New Year Mom 2020 69
Merry Christmas/Happy New Year Auntie 2020 70

Chapter 6   In Loving Memory 71
    Treasure of My Soul 72
    Superior Angel 73
    Spiritual Love 74
    See You Later in Heaven 75
    Raindrops 76
    Never Be the Last Kiss 77
    Missing You Grand Mom 78
    Lifted My Soul 79
    Janice Matrician 80
    In Spirit and in Your Souls 81
    I'm My Daughter's Angel 82
    Heaven's Stairway 83
    Harmony of My Life 84
    Don't Cry 85
    God's Palace 86

Chapter 1

CHATTER FROM THE HEART

Alone

We just called it quits after years together due to my infidelity
And it has made me lose my ladylove that completed my life
Because my past demons inside have caught up with me
And not seeking counsel back then has made me lose my love
I took the scandal from my marriage into this relationship
Like a hurricane storm brewing out in the open sea
Which caused me to think doing the same to my love
Now I am sitting here grimacing at the wall all alone

The loss of you has eaten away at my soul to the core
And it was driving me crazy every second of each day
Then I finally committed to talk to a professional Dr.
To help me open up about my past marriage history
Which played a major role in creating the monster in me
And after many sessions with the Dr. he found my distress
What he reviewed with me was that my pain was from my ex
Is that I never genuinely forgave her for her infidelity
Of having a child with another man while we were married
And opening up about that discomfort has me all alone

As they say things happen for a reason whether good or bad
And the bad thing I received was that I lost my ladylove
Because of the animosity I held inside for my ex wife
But as we chatted more about my feelings and my betrayal
The Dr. made me realize that my past grief manipulated my actions
Which caused me to take it out on the next person I loved in life
And that person was my ladylove which I crushed her soul
Actions speak louder than words and mine shattered our dreams
I sit here wishing that someday we can rekindle our romance
But until then I will lock myself away and sit here all alone

Amazing

Last night was so mind-blowing it will be hard to forget
As the vision of you keeps jogging through my mind
Even when I close my eyes your beauty is breathtaking
And when I fall asleep your warmth clutches my soul
Feels like I'm in a spaceship flying through hyperspace
My heart is jumping from left to right inside my chest
And I cannot control my addiction I feel for you
As the craving inside for you roars like a lion
Because what we shared last night was Amazing

Mornings come early when your mind is in the clouds
As my eyes get lost in the sun shining on your skin
Because caramel never looked so sweet and juicy
As you begin to rollover and slowly open your eyes
You smile, wink and blow me heart stopping kisses
As my hands begin to shake as the coffee spills
Then with the softness of your voice you say sorry
And I picture our adventure of last night that was Amazing

As you slowly wrap yourself up in the top bed sheet
And you lick your lips and raise the sheet up over your thigh
Eyeballing me up and down with that erotic glare in your eyes
Then you run your fingers through your hair as you walk away
But, as soon as you get into the doorway of the bathroom
You drop the sheet and ask me what am I waiting for
As you lean back outside the door with the look of a craving
Because you tell me that last night's opening scenes are not done
I hurry up to put the tray back in the kitchen to join you
As you are standing in the shower under the hot steamy water
And all of my enthusiasm of our passionate rendezvous is Amazing

As you dance and wipe away the steam from the shower doors
You commence to sing our favorite song as you motion me in
The divine sound of your voice builds nervousness within my core
And you leisurely slide the shower door open for me to join you
As you close us in as the steamy water runs tenderly over your body
My heart is beating 100 miles an hour listening to your sexy voice
Because you know what your singing does to me deep inside
Little by little you move towards me as you gaze into my eyes
And your voice has mesmerized me motionless and speechless
As you move in closer for the kill like a hunter stalking its prey
While my body is numb from the excitement and it's Amazing

The harmony of your voice and your body tingling touch is superb
As you have set my body heat above the temperature of the water
While I cannot resist the temptation with you standing close to me
I pull you into my arms as I kiss you one by one on your delicate spots
As you walk backwards up against the shower wall biting your lip
Because you know the tides have turned on the hunter inside of me
And the huntress in you is being tamed just like you like it
I know you are losing control as your body starts to twitch
Just as you brace yourself by digging your nails into my back
As you feel the flow of the water running through your fingers
And the script has been flipped on you and it's Amazing

The steam buildup inside the bathroom is beginning to thicken
And your kisses give me a taste of what's coming next
As you step up and anchor yourself on the ledge of the tub
While you gradually bite me upon my neck as you moan
Then you write those 4 words M.L.T.M. on the glass window
As you whisper in my ear you're ready as you lay your head back
I know this is going to be 100 times better than last night
And I take a firm grip of your backside in the palm of my hands
As I steadily run my tongue along your lips and down your neck
Until I reach the pinnacle of your breast that melts your soul
Because your body permeates with lust as this quest is Amazing

You wrap your legs around my waste as you pull me deep inside
And your muscles begin to quiver with every passionate stroke
As the water splashes just as you compel your fingers down my back
Because our uncontrollable appetite for this moment is astonishing
And our bodies are yearning for this moment right now to never end
While my mind is taking notes on how warmly my soul is attached to you
Because you have cemented your love in my heart I want forever
As we head into the final lap you commence to kiss my lips
And within seconds we both explode nonstop and it's Amazing

As My Heart Cries

We all try to find the love of our lives everyday
Because there is someone out there for all of us
However, as the years pass by it seems hopeless
I pray every night and hope she comes to me
Whether it is in my fantasies, dreams or by accident
At least one of them will give me the glimpse of her
I keep my faith knowing she is just a knock away
Because I'm hoping and praying that vision comes true
As I can't handle this loneliness inside my soul
Because my feelings begin to decay as my heart cries

Winter is holding our Spring with a ferocious grip
As the weather teases us with heavy winds, rain and sun
With the rollercoaster climates outside I remain upbeat
While my heart and soul are thirsting from deep within
For that beautiful woman to materialize before me
As she knocks me off my feet and seizes my soul
For the rest of my life to love and to hold forever
And when that day comes I will secure her in my arms
With bear hugs and sweet kisses to soothe her heart
As my life turns upside down as my heart cries

Beauty

As I sit here in the dark and listen to my heart
I hear the emptiness of my soul whispering softly
As I am waiting for that extraordinary lady to appear
Because all my life I acquired the opposite of my soulmate
And just when all hope seemed lost and impossible
Our paths crossed as your beauty opened and seized my heart
At that very moment, I felt like my life was rejuvenated
And we began to engage in conversation that blew my mind
Because I thought I was talking to myself in the mirror
Not realizing that we have so many connections alike
And not in a million years did I think it was possible
But that is what happens when you trust in God
And on this very day he sent you my beauty

Watching the movement of your lips as you talk
And the dimple in your chin just warms my soul
As your succulent chocolate skin jump starts my heart
And that gorgeous smile sends chills through my body
Because my world changed once you crossed the threshold
As you only read these types of stories in a fairytale book
But today God has graced my heart and my eyes to my own story
And his blessing has me stuttering my words I speak to you
Because he knows that this is not just a destiny but a prayer
And he sent me the love that I have been missing in you my beauty

Creative Souls

As we settle into our secluded beach front room
Just knowing that I'm with you is stupendous
But our thoughts this second will make it hot & steamy
Because as your robe drops around your ankles
And what you have on makes my mouth water
As my speech is slurred starring at your amazing body
Knowing what's in store will last all night until morning
As you slowly lay down on the bed with your back arched
Then you lift your head and lick your lips and blow me kisses
As you wink your eye and give me that I'm ready glare
And I begin to approach you with that sparkle in my eyes
As I gently march my hands up your legs to your thighs
Next up for us is the framework of our Creative Souls

You begin to squirm as I tenderly kiss you all over your neck
As I come up for air I see a tear running down your cheek
And you take both of your hands and grasp my face
While your sparkling glare pierces through my spirit
As more tears start rushing down your face like a waterfall
My heart melts as you softly tell me you love me for eternity
As I pull you close and say I love you beyond the stars
Then you lose control of your tears as I feel your heart racing
And the thirst of our love for each other sparks our Creative Souls

I have never felt love like this that is staggering at this point in my life
And holding you tight right now has hardened how much I love you
I can't hold my tears back anymore because you are my everything
As God leading you to me was like the last puzzle piece of my heart
To give me peace, comfort, love, and unity to complete my nucleus
As you raise my head up from your shoulder and kiss my tears away
The core of my soul begins to float beyond the stars in the sky
And your raving kisses are making my emotions mesh with your soul
Because you are the spark that ignites the love of our Creative Souls

Day & Night

Just finishing up work as my plans have been delayed
By the storm of dark clouds, high winds and lightning
That suddenly rolled in without any type of warning
Because I was looking forward to a walk on the beach
While the waves and sand run between my toes
So, I could clear my mind and focus on my life's worries
And all I can do these days is think of you day & night

When I wake up the thoughts of you run through my head
And when I close my eyes to go to sleep your still on my mind
These thoughts are constantly driving me crazy inside
Because I'm not sure what your motives are behind your calls
And since we have been apart for many years I'm losing control
Of my heart when it comes to you not being the woman in my life
Because I miss you lying next to me at night and in the morning
And all I can do is yearn for you every second all day & night

I finally had to write you an email to explain what I'm going through
Just to try and reset the core of my soul with the love I have for you
Because until I can pour my emotions and let you know my feeling
I won't be able to embrace all this turmoil that is intensifying in my heart
All of this is like the raging storm that is happening outside
The stress is resembling the waves crashing against the rocks
And all my heart and soul can do is ponder over you day & night

Dream Girl

They say that there is someone for everyone in life
Then we crossed paths and you confirmed that theory
Because starring into your eyes in this picture
Took me on a journey deep into your hurting soul
And what I uncovered inside gave me chills all over
It showed the good and bad within you for me
However, both made me scared and intrigued
Because honesty is great for us to explore together
But, at the same time I lean on God to send me a blessing
Can this be a bad nightmare or can you be my dream girl

Your eyes, lips and caramel skin exude exquisite beauty
Just knowing and seeing all of these qualities is scary
Because above average women over look average men
And my oh my you fit the bill of a true beauty queen
That would make any man who is smart fall in love
With your inner and exterior amazing magnificence
That God has blessed you with from head to toe
And I don't know if this is some type of daydream
If so let me stay dreaming and enjoy my dream girl

You say all the right things that has captivated my soul
And I continue to have some doubts in my mind
Because women of your attractiveness are never single
Just knowing you can have any man you want in life
However, you picked me and that is still hard to believe
Don't get me wrong by any means on being honored
Because you are a perfect woman to take home to mom
Which is that cherished queen that is my dream girl

Dreams

Winter time is knocking on the door
As the colorful leaves fall off the trees
And the crisp cool breeze soothes the soul
As Jack Frost is nipping at your nose
And the scent of hot cocoa warms the heart
As the fire place shines bright in the night
While keeping the blankets warm and cozy
So, I can hold my sexy queen oh so tight
As the time stands still in our minds
While we gaze into each other's dreams

Nothing better than sitting by the fireplace together
As the flames takes control of your mind, body & soul
While the blessedness of our future's stirs in our minds
As we wrap ourselves together under the warm blankets
Sipping on our cocoa as we fall into a trance for a second
As I turn to observe my loves succulent skin gleaming by the fire
And watching her mind wander and the different smiles on her face
As I can't get enough of ogling at her as she sits there so beautiful
Just trying not to disturb her while she is deep into her dreams

First Love (The One That Got Away)

As I walk along the river just staring upon the sunset
My heart aches beyond the sound of the riverboat passing by
All my mind is doing is reliving the time we first met
And I remember that moment in our lives like yesterday
I still smell the scent of your cologne you were wearing
And how so amazingly handsome you were in that suit
Because I everyone woman including me kept staring
But all I could think is that is a true man right there
As you inched closer & closer to the table I felt the energy
You possessed in your walk, as strolled through the crowd
As my soul & heart got lost deep within your presence
All I could think of is my first love (the one that got away)

The swift breeze of the river begins to bounce upon my face
As I begin to gently close my eyes your image appears before me
And I see those lovely eyes that hypnotized the essence of my soul
Because when we were together I never wanted to let you go
All I wanted to do is be stranded on a deserted island with you
Away from everything and everyone like we were shipwrecked
As you keep me safe, secure & caressed inside of your warm arms
And the connection we have made me feel like the world's only queen
Because what we had then was straight out of a fairytale story
Reminiscing of our love made me fall for you all over again
Because you were my first love (the one that got away)

Ghost of Love

My mind goes round, and round when I think of you
Because I know you belong to someone else
As I visualize you and me together forever
But that vision will always be an illusion
Because my soul yearns for you sincerely
And my heartbeats profusely inside my chest
While your smile sends chills throughout my body
And these feeling I have for you I cannot hide
Because every impulse for you makes me crumble
As my mind is haunted by the ghost of love

When you passed by walking across the atrium
And your voice made me turn to see who you were
At that moment you turned to initiate eye contact
My hands began to sweet as you smiled at me
And nothing even mattered at that split second
Until my friend bumped my arm and startled me
And then I found my mind fantasizing of you
But in reality the vision of you was just an illusion
Because my mind is haunted by the ghost of love

As I scoured the crowd to see if I was imagining you
My friends just shook their heads and said come on man
But deep down I was convinced you were truly real
As I started my drive home everywhere I turned
I pictured you walking to the corner of the street
And when I stopped at the light to look you weren't there
I sat there for almost 5 minutes trying to clear my mind
As the cars blew their horns heavily to move me along
Now I know my soul cannot withstand the ghost of love

I made it through the night for the first time in a long time
Without the vision of you haunting my dreams through the night
As this obsession is taking over the entire essence of my soul
And this fascination of you in my every thought has a hold on me
Because losing you in my life was beyond heartbreaking
And until I can make peace with your tragic passing
I won't be able to control these visions in my head
Because my soul is haunted by the ghost of love

I finally had the courage to go sit down in church again
To pray for grace and mercy over my soul to forgive myself
For you leaving me all alone and to go on without you
And I just began to uncontrollably cry sitting in the pew
Just blaming myself for not being able to save you my love
As I tried to handle this on my own to prove that I am strong
But losing you just made the core of my soul crumble inside
Then I felt a hand touch my shoulder and I looked up
And I began to gasp for air as the vision of your spirit
Set me free from all the loneliness and pain I was feeling
Because I was finally set free by the ghost of love

Great Picasso

As I roll over to hold you deep in my warm arms
I smell the succulent aroma of your perfume
That percolates off of my bamboo pillows
And your sweet scent captivates my soul
As it melts my heart and triggers goosebumps
Which runs through my body like a calm river
That sets off the butterflies in my stomach
As the vision of you next to me seems so real
Just as I lean over to kiss you on your shoulder
The alarm rings and snaps me out of my dream
And the vision of you in my mind is like a Great Picasso

Life can drive your mind and heart off of a cliff
Especially when you have to say goodbye forever
And today I know my faith has to be at its strongest
Because my tears just keep running down my face
Just knowing I won't have you when I need you most
As I collect my thoughts to hold it together today
Because my body is trembling nonstop uncontrollably
And my heart is breaking with every breath I take
As I drop to my knees to ask God to comfort me
While I have to say my goodbyes to my Great Picasso

God never puts more on your plate than you can handle
But today my plate is overflowing with sorrow
Because I will lay my ladylove down to rest forever
And I thought I would never have to bury her first
Nothing can ever prepare you for this moment
I just want to trade places with her right now

Because my heart is aching like it wants to burst
And the core of my soul feels like it is dying inside
My eyes are swollen like I went 15 rounds in the ring
From all of the tears that have soaked my carpet
Now I know what out of this world pain feels like
Because I have to say goodbye to my Great Picasso

If you have found that one woman that is in your life
That was your soulmate, best friend, wife and ladylove
Make sure you tell her how much she means to you daily
Because when you ever lose that amazing woman
It will put a strain on your heart like its hollow
And the agony you feel seems like you are suffocating
As it takes every ounce of breath out of your body
With a strangle hold on your soul that eats you alive
I pray my ladylove knows that her legacy will live on in me
Because she will be my everlasting life changing Great Picasso

Hands of Time

My mind is working overtime
Because all I can do is, think of you
It keeps playing tricks with my heart
As the hours, pass by slowly
Nevertheless, I know
I cannot wait for that moment
Because I will be with my baby again
To reminisce about those special moments
Laughing, running and playing in the rain
As we allow our souls to bond as one
To enjoy the Hands of Time

The sweet smell of the summer flowers is in the air
As I drive along the country side
While I listen to Classic Soul on the radio
To help me soothe my mind as I am missing you
I continue my drive until I reach the shoreline
As I pull up to get out of the car
I see a couple that reminds me of us
As they are walking along the sand hand in hand
Enjoying the Hands of Time

As I walk, along the coastline as the sun sets
While the wet sand slides in between my toes
As I stop and stare over the horizon
Because the view is almost as beautiful as your smile
And those amazing dimples that are heart stopping
However, nothing in this world can compare to you
Because, you have seized the essence of my soul
As I enjoy the Hands of Time

Heart Erodes

When you have demons inside of you that you let take hold
You can lose everything like love, your soul and your faith
Because the heart is not strong enough to fight the pain
And when the agony rises and the body trembles
At the essence of your soul as your inner core whimpers for help
Because the path of destruction that was caused by my demons
Made me lose and inflict pain on my ladyloves' heart
And not until I talked to a therapist did I realized my actions
Destroyed my ladyloves' spirit deep inside her fragile heart
And that pain traveled through her body and caused heartbreak
With an uncontrollable force that ravaged her beyond repair
Just because she seems strong on the outside her heart still aches
And it took my therapist to help me understand how her heart erodes

Years went by and I tried to keep her out of my mind once she left
But as long as I never heard from her or saw her it ate me up inside
And there was no one to blame except me for my selfish act of betrayal
Even though she moved on I thought she healed her broken heart
After all of these years of her being gone and in other relationships
Just recently she reached out to me and even stopped by for a visit
I thought she was happy being in a relationship with someone else
Not knowing she still didn't have closer from us being together
As I tried to apologize to her for the pain I caused her all these years
And I wasn't expecting her to forgive me I just wanted to say I'm sorry
Because I generated her pain, and suffering as her heart erodes

Over the years visiting with my therapist he told me how far I have come
To be a better person conquering my personal demons from my past
And how proud he was of me for admitting my faults to get well
But he also made me understand how much I truly loved my ladylove
And that I had two true loves in my life the first was my ex-wife
She caused all of my pain that made me hurt my second love
Which was my ladylove that I have lost forever and can't get back
But what I learned is that life can push you off a cliff
And it is up to you if you will survive the fall or ride the wind
To land on your feet to start over again with a clear mind and heart
But I will never ever stop loving my ladylove for as long as I live
And I will spend the rest of my life apologizing to her for the pain
That I caused her and I'm not asking for forgiveness from her
I just hope she can let go of the hurt and heal as her heart erodes

Joy

After a long work week full of stress and BS
I needed time to reflect and calm my psyche
So, I decided to check out the small bar downstairs
As I walked down through the lobby of the hotel
I heard this soft voice speaking at the front desk
As I looked over she was staring me down all over
Which gave me the chills throughout my essence
Like when you're a kid blushing in a candy store
It stopped me dead in my tracks heading to the bar
And the beam from her amazing smile lost me in time
The one thing I noticed her voice gave my soul joy

I turned my focus back to giving my mind peace & solace
After one of the most taxing work weeks this year
As I find the open corner at the bar to settle down
And I order a New York Sour to start off my night
Because this is just what my body needs to loosen up
Over on stage is this local smooth jazz band playing
As I lightly tap on the bar to the groove of the song
The bartender brings over my drink as I say thank you
She says to me that it looks like I needed this tonight
And she said this 2nd one is from the woman across the bar
As I look up it is the lady from the lobby which gave me joy

I raise my glass to her and say thank you from across the bar
As her amazing smile sparkles at me like a star in the night sky
I slowly walk over to ask if she would like to join me for a drink
And she said if it is not too much of a hassle for her to impose on me
I responded not at all and said her company is what the doctor ordered
Because it has been an intense work week and unwinding is a must
As I introduce myself and she tells me her name is Charity Wilks
And I take her hand and pull out the bar chair so she could sit down
The softness of her tone saying thank you shook my spirit within
Because my soul was mesmerized by the tenderness of her voice
And the calmness she has provided to my day gave me joy

I am a true believer that things happen in life for a reason
As we go back and forth conversing with each other
And the more I learn about her personality blows my mind
Because I have never met anyone like her before
I have been married and had many relationships
But none of them can measure up to this woman
And to compare them to her is not the right thing to do
Because only God can compare and judge us
But this woman has fascinating unique qualities
That I never thought was even possible in life
And one thing she has done is provided me joy

As the bartender came over as Charity went to the lady's room
And said to me that drink she sent me made an impression on me
Because the smoldering look on my face is beyond priceless
And she wished us the best of luck praying a relationship blossoms
With the biggest smile I said thank you & for making the drinks
And they helped us break the ice from meeting in the lobby to now
As Charity was walking back the bartender stopped her in transit
To whisper something to her and they both looked at me and smiled
And as she returned back I pulled her bar chair out for her again
I asked what that was all about and she said it's a woman thing
All I could do is smile & laugh because she unlocked my joy

I asked Charity if she would like another drink and she said yes
And I got the bartender's attention for two more drinks for us
As Charity placed her hand on top of mine and smiled
She said thank you for the wonderful time tonight
And she said meeting me made her feel warm & safe inside
Because she is normally shy and something took over her mind
To reach out to me and that is what made her look for me
And when she seen me at the bar she just had to break the ice
That is why she sent a drink over to me to get my attention
Because it seemed safer to do that than just walk up to me
And her telling me this made my soul melt with joy

Mind-Blowing

Today is the first day being in Hawaii living out a dream
As the sunrises over the ocean and shines through my window
I roll over to give my love a kiss and say good morning
As she begins to yawn and stretch from under the covers
And then she shows a soft grin over her shoulder
While licking her lips and winking at me with desire in her eyes
At that moment her actions made me melt like butter inside
Because this is my queen, my spark, my wife and my love for life
Then she soothingly rubbed her finger tips down my shivering back
She just has that special touch that sends my body into a convulsion
Every time she lays a hand on me with holding my hand or a kiss
And what I feel is like being on cloud nine and is so mind-blowing

My ladylove just loves knowing that she has that effect on me
And I can't imagine anything better than how that makes her feel
Because to me I'm always under her irresistible spell
And nothing warms my heart more than her captivating smile
I never thought my baby would open my soul up with just a touch
As it was on our wedding day watching her walk down the isle
Was like living a dream to me that somehow came true to me
And I had never in my life been so nerves, jittery and speechless
In all my life as she stood in front of me wanting to be my wife
That day was so extraordinary for me to enjoy and mind-blowing

My Future

My mind, body, and soul are feeling sorrow
As the darkness is overwhelming my heart
And I don't know if I can conquer this worry
That is flowing like a river inside of me
Looking at each day as it will be my last
If I cannot free myself from the devils grasp
Please God give me the strength to rise up
And loosen my soul from his evil clasp
As I put my belief and faith in you Lord
Please, cleanse my entire soul with you love
And the blessings you have in store for my future

My Queen

My mind is overflowing with thoughts of you
And with each vision of you makes my heart race
As I imagine running my fingers through your hair
While I kiss you gently along your neck and shoulder
And slowly massage your back with passionate strokes
Because my body is beginning to lose all self-control
As I scoop you off your feet and stare into your eyes
And move in leisurely to kiss those sexy juicy lips
Which cause fireworks deep inside my bodies core
Oh, what a burning feeling that runs through my veins
That makes my heart skip like I'm 12 all over again
Because there is nothing more I savor than you my queen

As I carry you to the bedroom and place you down on the bed
You begin to lick your lips and my knees begin to shake
Because your elegance has apprehended my mind and body
I commence to remove your shoes from your sexy feet
And I begin to rub your feet as you lay back on the bed
As I move in closer to lick you from your toes to your thighs
Which causes you to arch your back and spread your legs
At that point, I begin to move inside your thighs to your clit
And my nature begins to rise as my tongue glides over your skin
Because the only thing on my mind is to satisfy you my queen

Pain in My Soul

Have you ever felt like you are all alone in the world?
The pain you encounter day in and day out is excruciating
It seems like there is no end to feel like you're gaining traction
On how friends and family make you feel like an outsider
I try hard to hold onto God and my faith to see me through
And that seems like a heavy burden to carry on my heart
When you try to be the light in everyone's overcast day
As you realize that no one ever considers how you feel
Or take the time out of their busy schedule to check on you
It can erupt like a volcano and initiate the Pain in My Soul

It doesn't matter if you have a big heart to show love for everyone
Somehow that is never enough to help you feel like a part of society
And that becomes such a lonely place to be within your soul
It makes you feel like you are walking through a dark cave
With nothing but your dim flash light and no extra batteries
And nothing but the jacket on your back looking for an exit
As you follow the pathway and the echo of your footsteps
Bounce off the walls of the pathway you are following
Because you are left behind alone in the dark to find your way
And the chill of the darkness makes me feel the Pain in My Soul

As the light in your heart slowly fades into the darkness
I drop to my knees to pray to God to give me the strength
And the courage to draw His love for me to defeat this pain
That flows through my spirit and my soul that feels like the abyss
Just hoping He will shower me with His grace and mercy
To anchor my aching heart to continue on and find the light
That will jumpstart my faith once again to carry me through
So, I can build on His prayers for me to shake the Pain in My Soul

Part of My Soul

Together we have seen marriages and divorces
As we watched our kids grow and encountered sicknesses
But through all and all we stood by each other's side
As they say God put people in our lives for a reason
And if I stare in the mirror I see you as my image
Because our minds intertwine like the prettiest mirage
But the amazing thing is that it's more real than a pot of gold
At the end of a rainbow on a rainy day in the summer
And for over 25 years we bonded stronger than sisters
Because we know each other's thoughts deep within
And that makes your heart Part of My Soul

Please God Heal Me

Every time I hear from you it gives me chills inside
Then I can't get you off of my mind for weeks at a time
And it drives me crazy to the point I can't focus
On anything but you every second of a 24-hour day
I lose total control of my emotions as the tears flow
As I miss you beyond measure deep within my very soul
I try to fight these feelings clouding my thoughts
But for some reason you have subdued me from head to toe
And I am begging & pleading to find a way to let go
Please God Heal Me

Just as I gain control of my numbness when thinking of you
I get a text, or call from you & the cycle begins all over again
My heart and soul just can't take this stress much longer
Because my love for you is deeper than the depths of the ocean
If I don't get a grip on this soon I will lose my mind forever
And when that happens my life will be in a tornado vortex
Just knowing the unknown with you and how you feel
About me and if you have the same thoughts and feelings
Towards me running through the core of your essence
Dealing with the unknown with you is nerve-racking
Please God Heal Me

Roots of My Essence

I sit up on the side of the bed gathering my thoughts
Preparing myself to begin the day with a prayer for my love
As she is away overseas handling business for work
I stand up to stretch to go jump in the shower
And the water gushes over my face to wake me up
The perfect song pops in my mind and I pause for a minute
As I close my eyes and let the water run down my back
And I take a deep breath to recollect being apart from my lady
Missing the sound of her voice in the morning as we get ready
After being together for 25 years seems like just yesterday to me
And still today she makes me feel like we just went on our first date
Just knowing that fiery torch for her still burns deep inside of me
And that is why my passion for her is etched in the roots of my essence

As I head to the bedroom to get dressed to grab my coffee
I turn on the tv to watch the news to begin this lovely day
The only thing missing is my ladyloves morning hugs & kisses
And just the thought of them is still earth shattering to my soul
As I fix my coffee and sit down to eat my toast and fruit
A story comes across the news that attracts my complete attention
And what I see is staggering to see posted on multiple billboards
Is a dedication to me from my ladylove for our milestone anniversary
Wishing me an amazing 25th anniversary with our wedding picture
And telling me how much she loves me and will see me soon
I almost choked on my toast and things like that is why I love her
And that is why my passion for her is etched in the roots of my essence

My ladyloves dedication surprise is beyond miraculous to me
And I hope my 25th anniversary surprise can compete with hers
As my cellphone rings and it's my ladylove telling me happy 25th my love
And goes on to ask me if I had seen my anniversary surprise on the news
I can't even get my words together because I am just speechless
As I take a deep breath and answer her with a yes and a big smile
Knowing this is the beginning of a fascinating day for the both of us
As I hang up with my ladylove I head out to the studio for my surprise
I stop and pick up my parents and her parents to prepare for her treat
As we arrive to the studio and gather with our wedding party
We start to set up for the recreation of our wedding day on set
I facetime her maid of honor that is with my love on business
And shows me the layout of the church I rented overseas
And sent the pastor, makeup artist to be with my love & maid of honor
As this shows my passion for her that is etched in the roots of my essence

We have finished with the studio decorations and changed into our attire
I would love to see my ladyloves face when she opens her big gift
And can't wait to see how beautiful she looks in her anniversary dress
As I wait for the text from the maid of honor to stream them in live
30 minutes later I get the text ready to get this anniversary day started
My studio dials the maid of honor & the pastor into the big screen
I know she is stunned & surprised to see her dad standing there
Ready to start walking her down the aisle arm in arm once again
While our favorite love song begins to play in the studio & in the church
As her eyes are filled with tears just waiting to run down her face
Her dad is holding her close to him because she is trembling all over
And at that very moment our eyes intertwine our souls all over again
Just like 25 years ago as we gave our lives to God as being united
My soul still sobs for her and that is etched in the roots of my essence

As the smile and tears on her face speaks volumes about her love for me
And she is so blown away by on how much imagination I put into this
Because she couldn't stop saying in the screen oh my God constantly
And she wasn't letting go of her dad for any amount of money
As she closed her eyes to breath in and out to calm her nerves
The family gathered with me all told her to take her time
As we had nothing but time to consummate this moment together
Because the twinkle in her eyes would be everlasting in her heart
And I knew once again on our 25th anniversary I touched her soul
Just like when we pledged our lives to each other 25 years ago
Today we are devoting our lives all over again as Mr. & Mrs.
As my love flourishes for her as it is etched in the roots of my essence

Chapter 2

ACKNOWLEDGEMENTS

Farewell

It seems like yesterday we became friends and then family
As the hours countdown for your last great hoorah
And you will be leaving the company for good
I now know that God has been truly good to you
And that He has given you the best of both worlds
Because He has blessed you with your wishes & dreams
And I am honored to have you in my life sis
I am trying to control my tears right now
But I know this is not the end but a new beginning
And I will always be grateful for you in my life
Because God has given me a savior to my soul
And you have done wonders for me on many things
However don't ever forget me at any cost in your journey
Because when I build my legacy with my books
Always know you helped me stay humble
And I will truly miss our daily talks & walks
I will end here so I don't get to carried away
But I will miss you and love you lots!
God Bless You and Farewell!

Grandpa

My first grandson was born to the parents of Brittany & Keenan
On this day July 19, 2022 my glorious emotions took over my heart
And the second half of my life rejuvenated by your precious face
I haven't felt this much joy in my life since my son Keenan was born
And I sat still for a while just letting my tears flow down my face Amari
My entire soul twinkled through my eyes with God's everlasting love
Because I couldn't wait to hold you in my arms for the very first time
And when I held your tiny body in my arms I knew I was in love
Your precious soul captivated and elevated my entire heart
I couldn't stop smiling from ear to ear with the joy of you Amari
The emptiness that was in my heart has been filled with your existence
And I pray that God's grace and mercy allows me to watch you grow
I can't wait for the day that you will be able to call me Grandpa

Love You more than life itself "Amari Christopher"
Proud Pop-Pop, & Grandpa

Sisterly Love

Words can't explain 100% of my soul's thoughts
Because God gave me not 1 but 2 sisters to love
And I am beyond grateful, humbled and thankful
For you both for accepting me as part of your family
In today's world you rarely get that type of support
But you both have given me more than my fair share
And I have cherished every moment of each day
Because you both have offered me your Sisterly Love

Sending you my thoughts and prayers
God Bless & Love You Both

My Brothers

I look at the lives that all of my brothers have built
From being bankers, authors, artist, and business owners
And it makes me proud to see such strong men
Cherishing the ups and downs as you became successful
I just want to raise up, and say I am your biggest fan
Because each of you have shown me how to grow
As a man, a person, a friend, a brother, a son and a father
Nothing has made me more grateful than all of you brothers
I couldn't ask for better men as role models in my life
And I am truly grateful, and thankful for each of you
If I haven't told you all before I'm telling you now
I am proud, and blessed to call you My Brothers

Single Women on Valentine's Day

Let me not forget all the single women on Valentine's Day
Just because you are single doesn't mean you're not loved
It just means your heart is waiting for that special gentleman
That will be on the same level as your heart requires & desires
So, I want to take this time out and give you your roses now
And kneel down and celebrate all the single women on this unique day
I want you all to know you are cherished 365 days a year
Because no woman should be limited to a few special occasions
On such days like birthdays, anniversaries, and Valentine's Day
Because every woman is worthy of many more praiseworthy dates
So, all the single women stand up & give yourself a round of applause
As I line each of you up and personally bow down to you all
And hand out roses to each of the single women on Valentine's Day!!!

Lovely Feet Valentine's Day

After all of these years that have passed us by I still love your feet
They always capture my attention just like the first time we met
Seeing you walk away toward the bathroom in your mule slides
Just mesmerized me the entire time until you return to the table
And just seeing them recently brought back those butterflies inside
Because I could lick my lips and stare at your feet from day to night
And just thinking about them makes my temperature rise like a fever
But I know it is just my soul panting to have them touch my body
As it would cause me to want to caress your body from head to toe
Just knowing that it's not possible to get that close ever again
It will never ever stop me from holding on to those amazing memories
I want to wish you a very special lovely feet Valentine's Day!

Sending you an abundance of hugs & kisses
Happy Valentine's Day

Happy Retirement

Meeting you was like planting a tree that grew in my soul
With the many hours, months and years of laughter
You made me feel like family without saying the words
And my heart is crying inside as you head off into the sunset
But I know we will keep in touch every now and then
One thing I can say is that you will be forever in my prayers
Because you are not just a friend you are family for life
And today you make your farewell tour towards retirement
Always remember that you will be missed beyond measure
I am grateful and blessed for you to be a part of my heart
Thank You for accepting and allowing me to be in your life
Congratulations and best wishes on your Retirement!!!

Best Wishes on the next exciting chapter of your life!
Sending lots of love and hugs to you Vickie Stoker

Happy 19th Anniversary

Stars shine, the moonlight is bright and you're my life
Because 19 years ago today we fell genuinely in love
As God aligned the core of our hearts to beat as one
On this very day we said I do with our souls intertwined
Never neglecting to hold, comfort and love each other
Because our prayers had been answered for an eternity
And our lives will forever be blessed together as a whole
Not taking for granted our special bond as husband & wife
We will make each day count better than the next endlessly
As we stand here and celebrate with family and friends
I just want to Thank God for our glorious union

Chapter 3

BIRTHDAY CELEBRATIONS

Happy Birthday Shekita

You are celebrating your 32nd birthday year
With co-workers, family and friends today
We want to help you cherish this day
And make this birthday truly special to you
Thank you for allowing us to share this moment
As we pray that this birthday is better than the last
And God has blessed you with another year
As we shout out to the world in honor of you
Wishing you a fabulous Happy 32nd Birthday!!!!!

Happy Birthday Mom/ Grandmom/Great Grandmom

Today you celebrate another blessed year that God has granted you
It's not just your birthday you have been blessed with two great grands
God is good all the time and all the time God is good to you
Words cannot express how grateful, thankful and blessed we all are
To not only have you here to celebrate another wonderful year with you
As you enjoy your son, grandson and his wife, & great grandkids as well
Today is your special day but we all want to wish you a Happy Birthday!

Happy Birthday!
We All Love You!
From: Lester Jr., Keenan, Brittany, Santali, & Amari!

Happy Birthday Auntie 2021

As I write this through all the tears running down my face
I know only God can express to you how much I love you
Even putting the essential words together will not be enough
Because you have showered me with love I didn't deserve
And God blessed me with you to be my shining angel
To comfort me when I feel like there is no tomorrow
And that life may bestow hurdles for you to leap over
But as long as you have someone in your corner
You can get through all of the devil's challenges
That try to take over your life, heart and soul
And God doesn't give his strongest soldiers that burden
Because you can't handle it, he gives you that warm spirit
That comes from your angel which is what you are to me
To give me advice, comfort, lend an ear and the love
I need to hang onto the love of our Lord Jesus Christ
And I just want to Thank you and celebrate you
As I wish you the greatest blessed Birthday ever!

Love You more than words can express!
Happy Birthday Auntie!

Happy 50th Birthday Cuz

I searched the dictionary for the word that best fit you
And the words I found inside just wasn't enough
Because to me you are what a man symbolizes
A father, dad, husband, grandfather, son, brother and family
And with each one of those titles has a story spanning 50 years
Because you have giving so many memories to each of us
So, tonight I thank you for the love and the memories
That you have giving me to cherish and honor forever
Happy 50th Birthday cuz!

Love you cuz!
#WP4L

Happy 50th Birthday Dex

We met 36 years ago during the summer of 1983
You accepted me as not only a friend but a brother
And standing here today celebrating your 50th
Is a milestone that characterizes your amazing life
And the accomplishments you have experienced
I couldn't ask for a better brother and man
To be a part of my life and to call my brother
Happy 50th Birthday Big Bro

Love you my brutha from anutha mother
Happy 50th Birthday Dex
#WP4L

Happy Birthday Mel

Like the stars that shine bright in the midnight sky
And the sunrise that wakes you up every morning
Only God controls everything in your life
Because He has allowed you to cherish 50 years
To share with not just family and friends
But with all of the angels staring down upon you
May God's mercy and grace gloss over your soul
As you celebrate this milestone in your life!

Happy 50th Birthday!
Love you Mel

Greatness Offering Dreams

Angels come in all forms of life that we adore
Nothing can ever match the blessing of my angel
Because she is the strongest angel of them all
And I thank God for her daily because I love her
As she helped me grow from a boy to a man
With her tough love and amazing heart of gold
And when my days are daunting I think of her
Knowing that she wouldn't let me ever quit
As I can hear her say boy I taught you better
Than to let the devil take control over you
And I will always be your shield in prayer
Because she is my Greatness Offering Dreams

Happy Birthday Mom
Love you always your Grandson

Chapter 4

MOTHER'S DAY

Happy Mother's Day to My Daughter

Hello my darling daughter it's been a while for us
I just wanted to stop in and give you a hug and kiss
Because I hear your heart hurting inside of mine
And God is taking this time to comfort your soul
As he frees your mind of this pain and suffering
So, you can remember my life and dream of me forever
Because my spirit will wipe away all of your tears
Just to watch that beautiful smile glow on your face
And I am so proud of you through the good and the bad
Because you are stronger than you allow yourself to be
And my darling daughter mom loves you beyond the stars
Thank you for your endless love on Mother's Day!

Happy Mother's Day Mom 2020

Even though the world is experiencing turmoil
I am blessed to still be able to celebrate you
Today marks another Mother's Day together
And I pray that this day is better than last year
Because fancy gifts and elaborate dinners are terrific
But those things couldn't express enough of my love for you
So, I hope that this personalized keepsake tells the story
As I use the gift from God that He blessed me with
To pour out my heart and soul on Mother's Day for you
Thank you for sharing this special day of yours with me
Wishing you another amazing Mother's Day!

I Love You Mom!
Sending you abundant blessing on Mother's Day

Happy Mother's Day Grandmom 2020

2020 what a year this has started out to be
But all in all, we are here sharing this special day
Once again for another gloriously blessed year
You have shown me what it is to be a child of God
Just with your character, strength, love, and courage
Because you always face the world without fear
All of these traits are engraved deep within my soul
And I will cherish them until God calls me home
But until then I will pay tribute to you on this day
To wish you a lovely and Happy Mother's Day!

I Love You Grandmom!
Sending you abundant blessing on Mother's Day

Happy Mother's Day Auntie 2020

Words flow through my veins like the lifeline of my soul
And when this day comes around each year I get choked up
Just knowing that I get to express my feelings for you
As the tears fill up in my eyes while typing these words
I pray that they don't sound selfish or stupid together
Because it is hard to keep focused wiping tears away
But I know God would have never given me this gift
If He knew that I couldn't handle speaking from the heart
So, today he allows me to display my soul to you
As I wish you an extraordinary and Happy Mother's Day!

I Love You Auntie!
Sending you abundant blessing on Mother's Day

Happy Mother's Day Mom 2021

It's been 50 years today that I celebrate you mom
On a day that they label today as Mother's Day
But this is not the only day you are cherished
Because you are honored 365 days each year
We have had our ups and downs together
And God has weathered the storms with us
He has covered us with his grace and mercy
To keep us safe, healthy and strong through it all
And I Thank our Heavenly Father for you
I love you mom and I wish you a Happy Mother's Day!

Love You Mom!
Sending you an abundant of blessing on Mother's Day

Happy Mother's Day Grandmom 2021

I know that life has not been easy for you mom
But watching you over the years you made it
You walked by faith and not by the sight of the world
And you have been an inspiration to us all
Mother's Day only happens once a year
But I love you all year long beyond the stars
And God's grace has granted us another year
To appreciate His blessings for you today
I pray you have a Happy Mother's Day!

I Love You Grandmom!
Sending you blessing on Mother's Day!

Happy Mother's Day Auntie 2021

Whether the sun is shining or the rain is falling
It doesn't change the narrative for Mother's Day
This is a day to share my thoughts and feelings
And to let you know that I love you very much
I hope today brings you much joy, peace and happiness
Because God has blessed you to share this day with me
And I Thank Him for the best auntie ever created
Because you keep me going when I feel lost
And you have been a blessing in my life
Another year another celebration in your honor
I pray that our Heavenly Father comforts you
With love today for Mother's Day!!!

Love You Auntie!
Happy Mother's Day

Happy Mother's Day Mom 2022

Heavenly Father, Thank You for my mom's undying love for me
Mom, I know that raising me was not easy and I made it tough on you
As I got older and look back it was your tough love that saved my life
Because I could have been in jail, on drugs, and worse of all deceased
And God gave you the strength of His loving hands to weather the storms
To carry me on your shoulders and get me to the finish line of adulthood
If I have never told you of how grateful I am for your saving grace
And nothing I can ever do will be enough to repay you for loving me
All I know is that you have to travel through the greatest storms in life
To grasp what a mother has to endure to survive with being a parent
Let me just say Thank You for giving me a fighting chance in life
I pray that God bestows upon you tranquility, & love this Mother's Day!

Love You Mom!
"As one whom his mother comforts, so I will comfort you." Isaiah 66:13
Happy Mother's Day

Happy Mother's Day Grandmom 2022

Because you have always been my all-time greatest hero in my life
You belong in the conversation with the greats like Maya & Rosa
And the thinking picture reflects on how much you are on my mind
As you cry I cry, when you hurt I hurt, and when you smile I smile
What a wonderful blessing you are that has been engraved in my soul
I would travel through the devils playground to rescue you from harm
With God as my witness words cannot describe how much I love you
As He blesses you today, so we can continue to make memories together
I pray that God 's angels continue to encase you with His favor & love
Heavenly Father, award this young lady an amazing Mother's Day!

Love You Grandmom!
Happy Mother's Day

Happy Mother's Day Auntie 2022

Thank You God for blessing me, and my cuz for making this possible
So, we could share this picture with his mom and my auntie
Because life is getting shorter with each passing day in our lives
And making unforgettable and lasting memories are special to me
My heart, and soul aches in my life beyond your grace and mercy
I just pray that I can continue to put a smile on her face forever
With your blessings each second, every minute, an hour of every day
Because God you continue to wake up this temporary vessel of mine
As you allow me to shine and shower my auntie with love always
Heavenly Father, warm her heart this Mother's Day with your spirit
And comfort her soul with an abundance of everlasting love & blessings
Praying for heavens joy, peace, mercy and grace upon you today
Love you more than what my life is worth Happy Mother's Day!

Love You!
Happy Mother's Day

Chapter 5

MERRY CHRISTMAS/ HAPPY NEW YEAR

Merry Christmas/Happy New Year Mom Lynch

2021 has been a challenging year with losing loved ones
And the 1st holidays without you just won't be the same
Because I will never hear your voice or call my name
Ever again only in my prayers, memories and dreams
If I could turn back the hands of time just to say I love
As you laugh at my jokes with your warm heart
And to see your smile as you tell me boy you so crazy
Because the Holiday's, and your Birthday going forward
Will never be the same to your son from another mother
I know you hear the sadness that is flowing through me
As my heartbeat is throbbing and my eyes gushing with tears
I want to say Thank You and I Love You for accepting me
Just know that your love you shared with me was golden
And I will fill the hollowness in my soul with memories of you
Because your presence in my life lifted my spirit beyond the stars

Rest in Heaven Mom Lynch
Love you for an eternity!

Merry Christmas/Happy New Year Kesha

We have come along way together sis over the years
I would not trade you in for anything in this world
Because you continue to give me courage to strive for more
And I love you for always having my back through adversity
I'm never shy for words, but today the frog in my throat
Has me all choked up inside to express my love for you
I pray that you have a wonderful holiday season sis!

I Love You Kesha!
Merry Christmas and Happy New Year!

Merry Christmas/Happy New Year Tonya

We have traveled through the eye of the storm together
And you have been my bestie for as long as I can remember
Today I cherish you during this holiday season
With lots of tears, hugs and love that can't be measured
Thank you for sharing your heart of gold with my soul
I am truly appreciative of the love you have for me
As we close out 2020 with all of the challenges
I pray you have an amazing transition into your 2021

Love you always Tonya!
Merry Christmas and Happy New Year!

Merry Christmas/Happy New Year Mom

2020 has been marred with ups and downs
And the love we share is joy in my soul
Your faith has built the foundation of my life
Because you have been my rock through it all
Nothing in this world can ever tarnish our love
I'm grateful, thankful & humbled to be your daughter
I want to tell you I Love You beyond the farthest galaxy
And want to wish you the best holiday season and 2021 ever!

Love you always and forever Mom!
Thank you for being a Blessing!
Merry Christmas and Happy New Year!

Merry Christmas/ Happy New Year Grandmom 2020

This has been a year that our hope and faith has been tested
But through it all you have never wavered away from me
Because your passion, love and believing in me is unmatched
God has blessed me with the world's greatest grandmother
And I know I haven't been the best of grandson's
But if I don't tell you enough I love you to the moon
You have given me a purpose in life with your strength
And your courage is a marvelous blessing from God
I just hope that someday I can be strong enough
To be able to channel your courage in my life's journey
I am beyond grateful, humble and thankful for your love
I pray that through all of the trials & tribulations of 2020
You have a Merry Christmas and Happy New Year!

Sending you an abundance of blessing this Holiday Season Grandmom!
I Love You beyond the farthest solar systems!

Merry Christmas/ Happy New Year Mom 2020

How time has blown by and standing here on 50 years
I don't know if I could have survived this long without you
Looking back over the years I smile with tears in my eyes
Because you raised me all alone for better or worse
But you never threw in the towel and gave up on me
During hard times you fought tooth and nail to stand tall
And that deserves God's highest honor filled with blessings
Thank you for hanging in there for me through it all
I may not have been the most artistic or smartest but you loved me
And I will always be beyond thankful, and grateful to you
Even with all of the turmoil and madness of 2020
I pray you have a blessed Merry Christmas and Happy New Year!

Wishing you peace, joy and happiness this Holiday Season Mom!
I Love You more than the sun can ever shine bright!

Merry Christmas/Happy New Year Auntie 2020

Thank you for always lending an ear and being there for me
I pray that God moves your soul to let you know I love you
Because you have been a savior for my sadness in my life
Without you I don't know where I would have ended up
And only God's grace and mercy from your prayers saved me
There is not enough money in this world that can ever repay you
You remain in my prayer's morning, noon and night
Because that is my payment to you for all you do for me
And I pray you have a Merry Christmas/Happy New Year!

Sending you Blessings for this Holiday Season Auntie!
I Love You more than words can ever express!

Chapter 6

IN LOVING MEMORY

Treasure of My Soul

The greatest gift was to watch you grow from a child to a woman
Because you provided me with incredible joy, love and strength
And I admired your determination you showcased the whole time
My source of pleasure was sitting back and watching your success
Don't ever forget that I will always love you day and night
When you feel sad, I will comfort your soul with my angel wings
Letting you know that my spirit lives within your heart
And that this is not saying goodbye, it is I will see you later
Because you are the key that unlocks the treasure of my soul

In Loving Memory of Leona Odum
Sending prayers to you and your family Veronica

Superior Angel

I'm a true believer that God puts people in your life for a reason
And that amazing person to me was you Mrs. Billie Cain
Life will never be the same without you here with us
I know God needed one of His greatest angels created more
No longer are you fighting through pain or suffering
Tears are being shed today; but not in sadness, but in appreciation
All of your family & friends are celebrating & honoring your life
And we are beyond grateful for God allowing us to share it with you
Because you have touched so many of our souls over the decades
Stars shine at night, but never shined as bright as your fantastic soul
I want to "Thank You" for sharing your enormous heart with me
Because without a shadow of a doubt you earned your wings
And I may be sad, but Heaven couldn't be receiving a finer superior angel

In Loving Memory to Mrs. Billie Cain
Sending my thoughts and prayers to your family

Spiritual Love

To all my lovely sisters, please hold back your tears for me
Because time will heal all the grief you have in your heart
And God will bring us all together again when the time is right
But until then my spirit is hugging each of you tight
Just to ease your sorrow to comfort your souls
If I never said I love you enough I'm truly sorry
God called me home because he needed me more
And God's kingdom is beyond amazing let me tell you
Hang on to the memories we shared in our lives
Because I will always cherish our Spiritual Love

In Loving Memory of Deacon Lester Outlaw

See You Later in Heaven

Let's sit and reminisce about our love for each other
I know this will be difficult for us as a family
But through this disheartening time in your life
Think about all of the rainy days we shared together
With lots of laughs, smiles, and big hugs collectively
Because I know right now you are asking why me?
Look at it this way God had a master plan for me
To touch each of your hearts and souls in a sad way
But this is not a sad moment it is a glorious event
Just making sure we stay strong as a family
And never ever forget that our Heavenly Father
Will never put more on our plate that we can't handle
Even if He calls one of His angels home abruptly
I know this is hard on you but say a prayer with me
And relish in the blessing God places in your heart
This is not goodbye this is see you later in Heaven!

In Loving Memory of Charles Marcus Allen
Sending my thoughts and prayers to the Shareef Family

Raindrops

God has called home another angel to watch over me
I am sitting here with my soul throbbing in pain
As my thoughts are traveling like the clouds in the sky
This seems like a dreadful nightmare I am facing in my life
But through the good and bad times I am missing you
While the memories of us together brings a smile to my face
And I know God will grant me His grace and mercy to be strong
With His love and comforting arms wrapped around me
And the memory of you will flow through my spirit forever
I will love you forever from the depths of my soul
As the tears gently stream down my face
They are the essence of your soul like Raindrops

In Loving Memory of Hubert L. Crump Jr.

Never Be the Last Kiss

As I am looking upon you right now my sweet lovely daughter
Lately there has been many tearful days and nights with you
And I know your heart has shattered into a million's pieces
Because you have been struggling with my sudden departure
I want you to close your eyes and think of our time together
And let God's hands and your prayers take control of your mind
As His blessings will cover you going forward in your life
And give you the strength to alleviate your pain over time
Because He bestowed upon me my angel wings to hug you
Every time you feel sad, emotional, lost and broken inside
When you sense a warmth around you that is me hugging you
Remember that you are my heart and soul forever and ever
And I will always love you my dear until the end of time
As the picture shows us together this will never be the last kiss

In Loving Memory of Deborah Christine Caruso
Prayers to you and the family (Mimi) Michele

Missing You Grand Mom

It's been eight long years ago that you have been gone
And it seems like yesterday that I said goodbye to you
Because you being gone is never going to be forever
As we will meet again when God calls me home
And all of the things we shared I miss every day
But my soul is hurting with all the memories inside
As my tears run down my face while my heart breaks
And if I could just have one last hug from you
It would ease my pain and soothe my soul
Because I know you are looking down upon me
And saying a few choice words in your own special way
Because your love was nothing but heartfelt tough love
And I could use that tough love from you right now
As my soul is shattering and I'm Missing You Grand Mom

Lifted My Soul

Hello my love! I know your heart is hurting right now
And this is not saying goodbye, this is until we meet again
I know this seems like the end of our journey together
But our Heavenly Father needed me more right now
Please wipe away those tears until we meet in heaven
And God called me home to prepare me for a bigger plan
My heart is aching for leaving you behind my forever love
Each passing day will not be easy for the both of us
Just remember God will shine down upon your soul
And provide the strength over your heart to be strong
You stole my heart from day one when we met
And for over 57 years you were my angel from God
My love for you extends beyond the farthest galaxy
For you I am grateful and your love Lifted My Soul

In Loving Memory to Deacon Lester Outlaw
Sending my thoughts and prayers to you Linda L. Outlaw

Janice Matrician

My loving daughter today I need you to stand tall
Even though we are saying goodbye until we meet again
I will continue to watch over you forever in life
As God, has called me home and presented me my wings
I will still shower you with my love and everlasting blessings
Because when you look to the stars I will shine brighter
Than a sunset glowing and sparkling over any horizon
And that will be my spirit talking to you my dear Shekita

In Loving Memory of Janice Matrician

In Spirit and in Your Souls

Our Heavenly Father has called me home to be with your mom forever
I am finally at peace, and free from all of the pain and suffering inside
And oh, what a sight to see up close and personal the pearly gates
God and your mom were standing their waiting for me with open arms
And the joy on our faces to be together again brought back memories
Like the day we first met, along with our first date, and wedding day
Me & your mom are always looking down upon you kids in prayer
Knowing that we have never been so proud of our two girls and two sons
The only thing we ask from all of you is please watch over each other
Take good care of our grandkids and our son-in-law's until we meet again
As I would say with nothing but the deepest love for all "Right On"
Wipe away those tears because we taught you better than that
God will keep us engaged in your lives in spirit and in your souls

In Loving Memory of Mom & Pop Bruce
🙏 Rest in Heaven 🙏
Author: Lester Witcher Jr.

I'm My Daughter's Angel

My precious daughter I am holding you in my arms
As I walk through the gates of Heaven right now
Don't cry because my soul is free from this world
And I am in the presence of our Lord and Savior
As you remember me think of the amazing times
We shared over the years that will keep you safe
I know this is hard for you, but pain leads to joy
And joy turns into blessings that shower upon you
With each and every tear that runs down your face
Remember I will always travel with you in spirit
Each and every day for the rest of your life
Because I'm my daughter's angel

In Loving Memory of Curtis Henry Cantey
Sending my thoughts and prayers to you Jodie

Heaven's Stairway

I see lots of tears being shed over my calling home
Please family dry your eyes because God needed me
And what your feeling inside doesn't change the pain
But when He calls we always obey His summons
Because His footprint on my life has been a blessing
And I want you to grasp onto our epoch loving moments
As you think of the adventures we accumulated together
How oh so breathtaking that made us feel inside
I know your heart is crying deep inside of your soul
But let God and me comfort you with our loving arms
As we wrap them tight around you and dry your soul
While you feel the eternal blessing in your heart forever
And when we meet again it will be at Heaven's Stairway

In Loving Memory of Charles Marcus Allen
Sending my thoughts and prayers to the Allen Family

Harmony of My Life

My dearest daughter Shanna keep smiling my baby girl
Because you were the greatest gift a mother can ask for
You brought so much joy, laughter, blessings, and love to my life
And standing here next to God I Thank Him for you everyday
Please, wipe away those tears of sorrow and turn them into joy
Because every time you think of me I'm not far just a prayer away
All this is just a test to show you how strong you have become
And if you stumble I will be there to catch you before you fall
Remember all of the amazing and beautiful times we shared together
Because you will always be the Harmony of My Life!!!

In Loving Memory of Debra Ellen Clark
🙏 Rest in Heaven 🙏

Don't Cry

Night and Day, I spoke to God to give me the words to say
And He touch my soul to let me know that everything is ok
As I know that both of your hearts are feeling broken inside
Just remember I am dancing in heaven next to our Lord Jesus
And He promises to watch over you both and comfort you
Knowing that this is not goodbye it is I will see you later
Because I know that God will bring us together all over again
And when that day comes I will cover you with hugs & kisses
His grace and mercy and loving arms will keep you safe
If you ever feel lost and alone remember I am just a prayer away
Because our time spent together recently gave us elite memories
And we will always share laughter, joy, tears and happiness
And what better way to say I Love You and Miss You
Please dry your eyes for me and please Don't Cry

In Loving Memory of Deborah Christine Caruso

God's Palace

God created the most amazing mom in this world
And He blessed our family with a precious rare gem
That birthed me, and taught me the lessons of life
There is not a mountain high enough for me to climb
Because she made sure that only God could stop me
Today I celebrate my birthday and my first Thanksgiving
Without my momma that I miss so much each and every day
As my eyes gloss over with tears from the depths of my soul
I can feel her warm loving arms holding me like never before
Comforting my pain inside and letting me know it will get better
As this is a first of many major holiday celebrations without her
God will sustain my blessings with the memories of my momma
While she still prays, loves & comforts me from God's Palace

In Loving Memory of Mom Shirley Lynch (Missing You!)

www.ingramcontent.com/pod-product-compliance
Lightning Source LLC
LaVergne TN
LVHW092056060526
838201LV00047B/1419